Why must I clean my teeth?

FOX EYE
PUBLISHING

Why do I have to clean my teeth?

Why?

Because cleaning our teeth will help to scrub away a bad bacteria called plaque.

Why is plaque a bad bacteria?

Because when we eat sugary and starchy foods it makes acid, which damages our teeth.

Why does the acid damage our teeth?

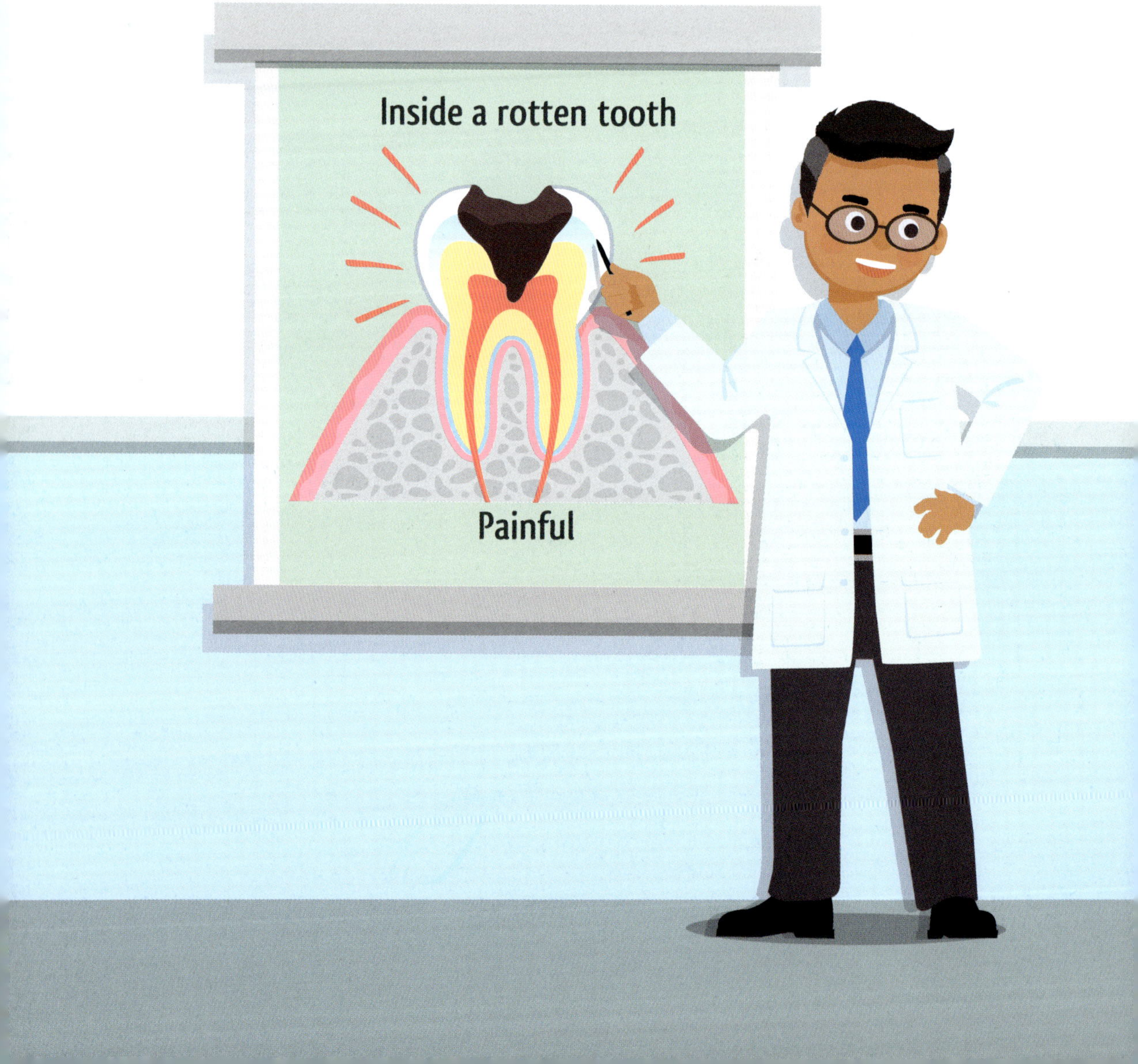

The acid makes holes in them. Over time these holes can get bigger and bigger until there is no tooth left!

Why don't animals have to clean their teeth?

Because most wild animals have diets that are low in sugar, and they chew on lots of hard things that help to clean the plaque away off their teeth.

Why doesn't Grandad brush his teeth!

Because his aren't real. He never used to clean his teeth when he was your age and now has to wear false ones.

Let's find out about Teeth

Turn the page over to discover the answers to these questions.

How many teeth do people have?

What animal has the most teeth?
What animal has the longest tooth?
What animal has the sharpest tooth?
Limpets have the strongest teeth. Stronger than Titanium.
What is so special about toothpaste?

Let's find out about Teeth

The answers are...

Children have 20. Grown ups have 32.

Sharks are constantly growing new teeth. They lose a tooth at least once a week.

60 but they lose their teeth a lot and will grow 2000 teeth in their lifetime.

Snails and slugs have the most teeth between 14,000 and 27,000.
The elephant has the longest tooth.
The Orca (Killer Whale).
Limpets have the strongest teeth. Stronger than Titanium.
Commonly, it contains a natural chemical called fluoride which helps to prevent tooth decay.

How to use this book

You can read this book with one child or a group of children.

The book can be used to begin a discussion around complex questions such as learning why we must brush our teeth.

The book is also a reading aid, with enlarged and repeated words to help children to develop their reading skills.

How to read the story

Before beginning the story, ensure that the children you are reading to are relaxed and focused.

Take time to look at the enlarged words and the illustrations, and discuss what this book might be about before reading the story.

New words can be tricky for young children to approach.

Sounding them out first, slowly and repeatedly, can help children to learn the words and become familiar with them.

Did you spot
the Tardigrade
hiding in
this book?

First published in 2023 by Fox Eye Publishing
Unit 31, Vulcan House Business Centre,
Vulcan Road, Leicester, LE5 3EF
www.foxeyepublishing.com

Written and illustrated by Simon Couchman

ISBN 978-1-80445-356-8

A catalogue record for this book is available from the British Library.

Printed in China

Titles in the Series

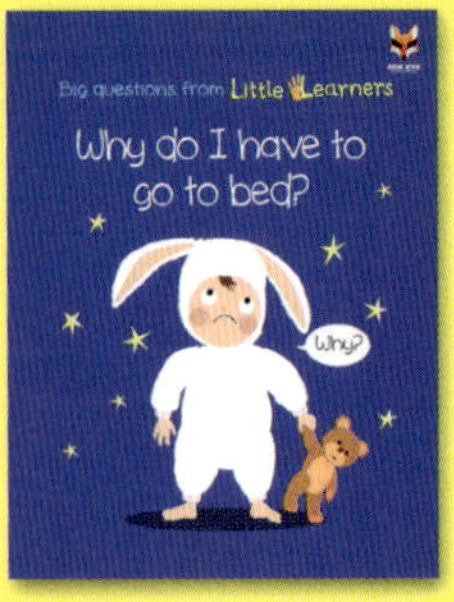

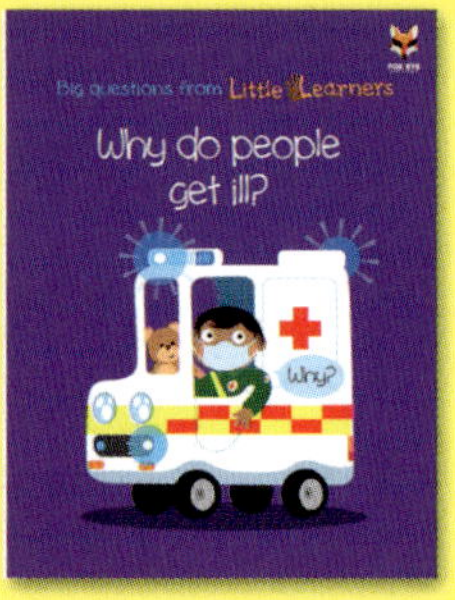

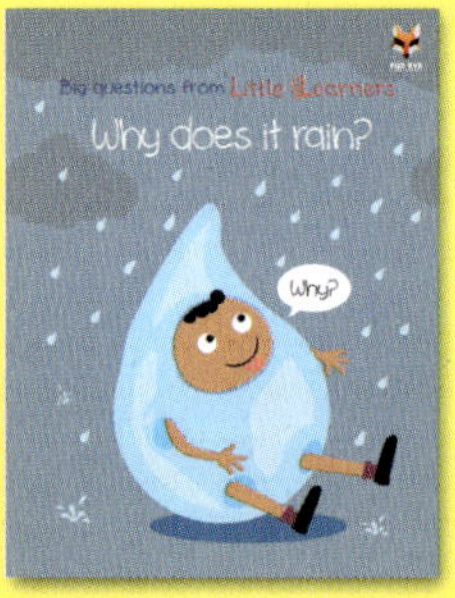

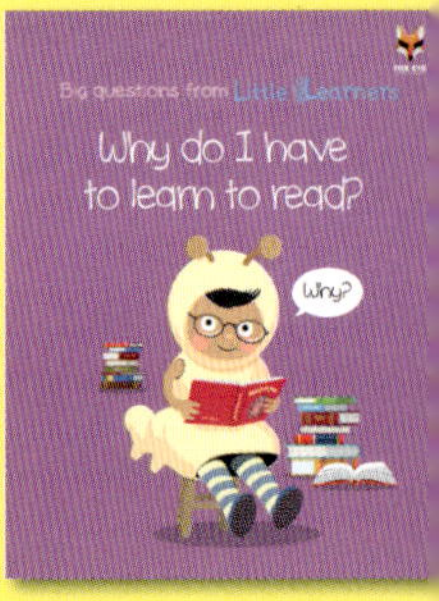

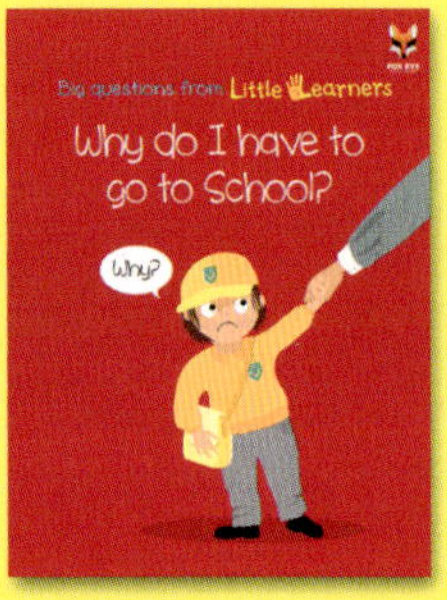